Crazy Textile Jewellery & other Accessories

Using Water-Soluble Stabiliser

Hannelore Koch

Crazy Textile Jewellery & other Accessories

Using Water-Soluble Stabiliser

Search Press

Contents

Foreword

Dear Reader,

People who love working with textiles are always looking for new inspiration and new challenges.

Water-soluble stabiliser is a magic material for creating something completely new. Its stability and transparency mean that a wide variety of techniques are possible. For the experienced textile-lover, it provides countless opportunities to be creative with all types of materials, and it opens up new possibilities for producing personalised fabrics.

With the help of water-soluble stabiliser, you can make unique pieces from self-painted silk fabrics, sewing and knitting yarns. From jewellery sets to tops and stoles, belts and handbags – by paying attention to detail, you can create some quite individual designs, using very little in the way of materials.

You'll soon develop a preference for specific forms and ways of working, coming up with your own ideas. The colour and shape of the items shown can be adapted as you wish.

Let both your imagination and your sewing machine run riot by creating your own artistic fashions and accessories for special occasions!

Hannelore Koch

works as an independent textile designer. She specialises in silk painting and in working with silk in fashions. Her unique work is characterised by innovative designs that make use of traditional handicraft techniques. Her creations can be seen at exhibitions and fashion shows – most recently in Madrid and Florence.

Materials

- crêpe satin in natural white (fine, shimmering silk for painting)
- chiffon in white (transparent silk fabric)
- silk paints, steam- or iron-fixed
- water-soluble stabiliser, e.g. Soluvlies by Freudenberg, 90cm (35½in) wide
- iron-on stabiliser, e.g. G 785 by Freudenberg, 90cm (35½in) wide, available in white, black and skin tone
- iron-on stabiliser, e.g. S 320 by Freudenberg, 90cm (35½in) wide, available in white
- double-sided adhesive stabiliser for appliqué, e.g. Vliesofix by Freudenberg, 90cm (35½in) wide
- yarns and wool (for laying on to the stabiliser)
- spray adhesive or temporary spray adhesive
- sewing thread (for use as top and bobbin thread on the sewing machine, various colours)
- sewing thread, spool embroidery thread (bobbin thread for the sewing machine, available in black and white)
- metallic embroidery thread (for use as top and bobbin threads on the sewing machine)
- beads and jewellery fastenings: glass beads in various shapes and colours, earring findings and necklace fastenings, etc.
- catches: hooks and eyes, press studs, chain fastenings
- bag handles

Water-soluble stabiliser – acts as a support for all types of embroidery. The stabiliser can be rinsed out even in cold water without leaving any residue. However, the manufacturer recommends water temperatures of 25–30°C (77–86°F) and above – depending on the technique and material used. The stabiliser can be ironed on and has very good stabilising properties when working with other materials. It enables you to embroider on very fine, transparent fabrics, without adding a top layer of fabric too. The stabiliser is transparent white, so that patterns – if drawn clearly enough – can simply be laid underneath and traced over with a graphite watercolour pencil.

Iron-on stabiliser – comes in a fine, two-way stretch elastic form and is ironed on to the reverse of the silk used. A firmer iron-on stabiliser is used as interfacing for bags, belts and caps.

Spray adhesive – gives the water-soluble stabiliser an adhesive surface, preventing silk decorations from slipping and enabling precise sewing and embroidery. Shake the spray adhesive well before use and spray at a distance of approx. 20cm (7¾in). Spray quickly and cover the fabric with yarn straight away or within the next hour. The adhesive effect will disappear without trace within two to five days, or when rinsed out.

Tools

Freehand quilting foot – used for many items in this book. For this freehand embroidery, the sewing machine feed dog is dropped down and the embroidery is freely guided by hand.

Darning foot – part of the standard selection for most sewing machines, can also be used for embroidery, but has a smaller opening than the freehand quilting foot.

Metallic embroidery needles – useful when sewing or embroidering with metallic embroidery thread. These needles have a larger eye and are designed for metallic threads. The threads do not break as easily as when using traditional sewing needles.

Graphite watercolour pencil – recommended for drawing lines and designs on to silk and water-soluble stabiliser. The lines can be removed from the silk or stabiliser. Never use a ballpoint pen or felt-tip pen, as the colour will penetrate the silk and cannot be removed later. An alternative to drawing is to use a ghost pencil, whose lines will fade over time (between four and fourteen days).

Watercolour pencil in white – this water-soluble pencil is needed for pre-marking dark fabrics.

- sewing machine
- sewing foot for straight stitch and zigzag stitch
- freehand quilting foot or darning foot
- metallic embroidery needles for the sewing machine
- hand-sewing needles: sewing needle, darning needle, bead needle for hand embroidery
- pins
- cutting wheel and firm cutting base
- dressmaking scissors
- graphite watercolour pencil (for drawing on water-soluble stabiliser)
- watercolour pencil in white (for drawing on dark fabrics)
- ghost pencil (lines disappear after a period of time)
- felt-tip pen and tracing paper
- silk painting frame, sturdy clear film or oilcloth (for painting the silk)
- paintbrush for silk painting
- steam-fixing machine (for fixing the silk when using steam-fixed silk paints)
- iron

These are the tools required for making all the items shown in this book, but are not listed again with the individual instructions.

Painting silk

Painted silk looks a lot more interesting and lively than silk dyed in one colour in a uniform shade.
Silk is painted using a simple wet-in-wet technique, where the silk is sprayed with water and then painted straight away with silk paint. Usually silk is stretched over a frame for painting. With small pieces of silk, sturdy clear plastic film is sufficient as a base. When painting with steam-fixed paint, the silk must be fixed in a special machine (some craft shops offer a fixing service); this is the process used for the items in this book. Iron-fixed paint is fixed by ironing. Afterwards, the paint residue must be washed out.

Materials

- spray bottle
- silk painting frame, sturdy clear plastic film or oilcloth
- wide, flat paintbrush (broad brush)
- silk paint, steam- or iron-fixed
- fixing machine for steam-fixing, or iron

INSTRUCTIONS

Dampen the silk using the spray bottle and stretch over a silk painting frame or lay on to clear plastic film or an oilcloth.

Using a broad brush, apply diluted paint evenly in a pale shade.

Create accents using a darker shade and allow the paint to run. The painting does not need to be exact, as the silk will later be cut into decorations and the colour-runs will fit well into the design.

Allow the paint to dry and fix the silk thoroughly (steam-fixing or iron-fixing). Steam-fixed colours tend to be brighter. Silk also does not fade and can be washed in cold water and dry-cleaned.

Finally, wash the silk and then follow the relevant instructions.

Designing and sewing

INSTRUCTIONS

Preparing the silk

To prevent the silk from fraying when cutting out, iron the iron-on stabiliser to the reverse. Quickly fix using a low heat, so that the silk does not lose its shape.

Cutting out the decorations

Cut out your own patterns by hand or transfer the relevant patterns and make templates from card. Draw the decorations on to the reverse of the prepared silk using a watercolour pencil and cut out (fig. A).

Preparing the stabiliser

Cut out the water-soluble stabiliser twice according to the cutting pattern. Cover the work surface, lay out one piece of stabiliser as a base and spray with spray adhesive.

Arranging the decorations

Arrange the silk decorations on the stabiliser and press down (fig. B). Spray with a very fine layer of spray adhesive; place the second piece of stabiliser as a covering stabiliser on top, without creasing, and press down.

Jewellery

Some of the jewellery pieces do not make use of silk, in which case transfer the pattern to the stabiliser using a watercolour pencil and place two to three layers of stabiliser underneath for stability. Stitch the sewing or embroidery lines through all the layers.

Sewing and embroidering

Using the sewing foot for straight or zigzag stitch, sew or embroider using the darning or freehand quilting foot and the sewing machine, with the feed dog dropped. Guide the work slowly by hand, but sew at high speed (fig. C).

Rinsing the stabiliser

Rinse out the stabiliser by hand under cold, running water until there is no residue. Add a little detergent for delicate fabrics. Leave the piece in the rinsing water for a little while. If there is still residue in the water, add a little fabric softener or vinegar to the rinsing water. Iron dry beneath a towel (fig. D).

Fire flower

Decorative collar and cuffs

This elegant decorative collar with matching cuffs is the icing on the cake for any party outfit. Flowers and leaves are cut from fiery red silk. As the collar and cuffs are made in the same way, we recommend that you work on both items at the same time.

Tip

Fashion items and jewellery made from painted silk are washable. Wash carefully in lukewarm water using shampoo; rinse and leave to dry on a towel.

MATERIALS

- silk satin 08, 75 × 80cm (29½ × 31½in)
- silk paint in red
- iron-on stabiliser e.g. G 785 by Freudenberg in black, 75 × 80cm (29½ × 31½in)
- water-soluble stabiliser, e.g. Soluvlies by Freudenberg, 150 × 80cm (59 × 31½in)
- spray adhesive
- sewing thread in black (for the bobbin)
- metallic embroidery thread in red (for the top stitching)
- glass beads in red:
  approx. 15g (½oz) rocaille beads,
  approx. 30 pyramid beads (diameter 6mm),
  approx. 65 facetted beads (diameter 4mm),
  approx. 8g (¼oz) bugle beads (7mm),
  approx. 40 drop beads (3mm)
- 7 press studs, 7mm

INSTRUCTIONS

Decorative collar

Paint the silk satin on the painting frame or on rigid clear plastic film, wet-in-wet, with red silk paint (see 'Painting silk', page 10). Then steam- or iron-fix the silk.

Place the iron-on stabiliser on to the painted side; quickly iron here and there on a low heat, then iron down smoothly.

Trace the patterns for the leaves and flower motifs (see page 14) and prepare the templates. Transfer the motifs on to the iron-on stabiliser side of the silk using a white watercolour pencil and cut out.

Cut out the shape of the collar twice from water-soluble stabiliser (see cutting pattern on page 56). Draw on the motifs using a graphite watercolour pencil or ghost pencil, or just use your own judgement.

Spread out a piece of stabiliser on the work surface, spray over it with spray adhesive and arrange the cut-out motifs on the stabiliser with the red silk side uppermost. Ensure that the motifs touch one another and overlap a little at the corners. Finally, press down firmly. Check the arrangement of the decorative pieces once again and change if necessary. Spray with spray adhesive, lay the covering stabiliser on top, without creasing, and press down. Leave the piece of work for a short while, so that the fresh spray adhesive does not clog up the sewing machine needle.

When sewing, use black sewing thread for the bobbin thread and red, metallic embroidery thread for the top stitching. Sew at a fast speed using the darning or freehand quilting foot, moving the fabric slowly by hand. Edge the motifs in little circles; embroider some leaves with veins. Sew a netting pattern in some of the large spaces in between by joining the motifs with lengthways and crossways stitching, like darning. With each line of stitching, make a stitch into the silk and then sew back over it.

Rinse out the piece of work in cold water and leave for a while in the rinsing water, allowing the spray adhesive and stabiliser to completely dissolve.

Finally, thread the bead fringes and sew on to the decorative collar. Decorate some of the flowers and leaves with beads. Sew on a press stud for the fastening.

Cuffs

The cuffs are made in the same way as the collar. Both cuffs should be made at the same time next to one another, so that they look the same (see pattern, page 56).

Once all the sewing has been done, rinse out the pieces of stabiliser in cold water and leave for a short while in the rinsing water, allowing the spray adhesive and the stabiliser to completely dissolve.

Sew three press studs on to each cuff to fasten them. If you like, you may also decorate the cuffs with red glass beads.

Tip

The collar and cuffs can also be quickly attached to a simple jacket using Velcro®, turning a daytime outfit into an evening one.

Miami

Halter-neck top

With its wide chiffon ribbon tied at the back, this glamorous halter-neck top will make its wearer the focus of any party. If you feel happier with your shoulders covered, you can make a matching chiffon stole and you could sew beads on to the ends.

Tip

If you would like to wear the top directly against your skin, but are worried that something might slip out, do what the film stars do and stick some double-sided adhesive tape to the 'strategically important' areas.

MATERIALS

- crêpe silk satin 08, in white, 75 × 80cm (29½ × 31½in)
- silk paint in turquoise and blue
- chiffon in white, 140 × 80cm (55 × 31½in)
- iron-on stabiliser, e.g. G 785 by Freudenberg in black, 75 × 80cm (29½ × 31½in)
- water-soluble stabiliser, e.g. Soluvlies by Freudenberg, 200 × 90cm (78¾ × 35½in)
- spray adhesive
- sewing thread in blue
- metallic embroidery thread in turquoise
- glass beads in blue:
  approx. 25g (1oz) rocaille beads,
  approx. 10g (¼oz) bugle beads (7mm),
  approx. 120 facetted beads (diameter 4mm)

INSTRUCTIONS

Paint the silk satin with diluted silk paint in turquoise (see page 10). Paint flowers and leaves in blue in the wet paint; the shapes do not need to be exact and the colours should run. Paint the chiffon in the same way using a mixture of blue, turquoise and water. Once dry, fix the silk and chiffon. Wash the fabric, iron and reinforce the silk with iron-on stabiliser.

Paint decorations on to the black stabiliser side using a white watercolour pencil and cut out. You can work either freehand or using the patterns on page 56. The two pieces for the top can be made separately – they do not need to look the same.

Draw the pattern for the top (see page 56) twice on to water-soluble stabiliser using a watercolour pencil, with the two pieces joined at the neck (fold); one piece acts as a base piece for the silk and one as a covering stabiliser. Cut out generously. Now spray the pieces of stabiliser with spray adhesive, cover with the silk decorations, spray fix again, press down and cover with the covering stabiliser (see page 11).

Sew using the darning or freehand quilting foot at high speed, but using slow turning movements. Embroider over the decorations in circles or in leaf-like shapes with metallic embroidery thread. Sew the spaces in between lengthways and crossways with blue sewing thread as if darning. Always attach a little to the silk. Carefully check that all the silk edges have been caught, before rinsing out the stabiliser in cold water. Leave for a short while in the final rinsing water. Lay out to dry, then carefully iron beneath a towel. Embroider individual decorations (e.g. leaf veins) and some of the netting areas with beads.

Sew two ties from the painted chiffon – 75cm (29½in) long and 35cm (13¾in) wide when folded in half – and attach to the sides of the top as in the pattern (see page 56). Before sewing on, adjust to the required size. Sew the two pieces to each other by hand along the centre front for approx. 15cm (6in).

Spanish night

Bolero

This little bolero jacket will always be eye-catching – no matter what colour or decorations are used! The variety of shapes makes it exciting to make. Floral motifs, geometric shapes or even the patterns on page 51 can be used to form the basic design.

Tip

When drawing on the motifs never use a ballpoint or felt-tip pen, as they will penetrate the fabric and cannot be removed later. Always use a watercolour pencil.

MATERIALS

- crêpe silk satin in white, 100 × 80cm (39¼ × 31½in)
- silk paint in blue and turquoise
- iron-on stabiliser, e.g. G 785 by Freudenberg in black, 100 × 80cm (39¼ × 31½in)
- water-soluble stabiliser, e.g. Soluvlies by Freudenberg, 140 × 90cm (55 × 35½in)
- spray adhesive
- felt wool (100% merino/new wool), 25g (1oz)
- microfibre yarn in turquoise/white blend, 25g (1oz)
- sewing thread in blue and turquoise

INSTRUCTIONS

Dampen the silk, dye the background in diluted turquoise/blue. Paint leaves and flower shapes on to the still damp silk using a darker turquoise and blue. The painting does not need to be exact and the colours can run. Once dry, fix the silk, rinse, iron and reinforce with the iron-on stabiliser.

Draw motifs freehand on to the black stabiliser side using a white watercolour pencil and cut out. Using the paper patterns for the bolero pieces (see pattern, page 57), work out the required number of silk motifs.

Transfer the pattern on to water-soluble stabiliser using a watercolour pencil: you will need two back pieces (folded) and a total of four front pieces. Adjust the size if necessary (size 12 shown here).

Lay out a back piece and spray on a very thin layer of adhesive. Place the silk motifs on top and press down. They should always overlap slightly. Cover the edges well, so that you can sew strong seams.

Now lay little tufts of felt wool on to the areas in between – not on to the silk. Lay the microfibre yarn on top in little spirals – mainly on to the felt wool and here and there on to the silk. Spray over with spray adhesive. Lay on the second piece of stabiliser and press down. Complete both front pieces as for the back piece; cover them at the same time, so that they look the same.

Sew closely – distances between the lines of stitching: 0.5–1cm (¼–½in) using the darning or freehand quilting foot at high speed, whilst making slow turning movements.

Cut off the water-soluble stabiliser close to the edge all round and sew up the shoulder and side seams. Wash in cold water and rinse several times, carefully squeezing out without wringing. Leave in the final rinsing water for a short while. If the work starts to stick, add a little vinegar to the rinsing water. Lay out to dry and iron on the reverse side if needed.

Blue planet

Jewellery set

You only need a really small piece of silk for this enchanting choker necklace with matching earrings and bracelet. There is no need for a painting frame either, as some clear plastic film or an oilcloth will serve as a base for painting.
It is best to make all three pieces of jewellery at the same time, so they will match one another.

MATERIALS

- silk satin 08 in white, 30 × 40cm (11¾ × 15¾in)
- silk paint in turquoise and blue
- iron-on stabiliser, e.g. G 785 by Freudenberg in black, 30 × 40cm (11¾ × 15¾in)
- water-soluble stabiliser, e.g. Soluvlies by Freudenberg, approx. 100 × 40cm (39¼ × 15¾in)
- spray adhesive
- sewing thread in blue (for the bobbin)
- metallic embroidery thread in turquoise
- glass beads in turquoise:
  approx. 15g (½oz) rocaille beads,
  approx. 30 pyramid beads (6mm),
  approx. 30 pyramid beads (diameter 4mm),
  approx. 8g (¼oz) bugle beads (7mm)
- 5 press studs, 7mm
- 2 earring findings in silver

INSTRUCTIONS

Necklace

Dampen the silk satin and paint in turquoise and blue (see page 10). Colour runs and rings add interest. Once dry, fix the silk, rinse, iron and reinforce with iron-on stabiliser.

Transfer the pattern for the necklace (see page 57) on to water-soluble stabiliser and draw on round shapes in various sizes, with diameters of 1–4cm (½–1½in) as in the photo; join with bridges. Cut out the relevant number of small and large circles from the reinforced silk.

Place the stabiliser, with the drawn shapes, face down on to light paper. You should still be able to see them clearly. Spray with spray adhesive. Lay the silk circles on top, colour side down, and press down. Spray again with adhesive, cover with stabiliser and turn over.

The drawn shapes are clearly visible. Sew over the round shapes in circular movements. After each circle, sew the bridge straight to the next one. A bridge consists of two lines of straight stitching and a third using small circular movements over the top.

Rinse out in cold water, iron dry beneath a towel, embroider with beads. Sew on press studs.

Bracelet and earrings

Draw the pattern for the bracelet on to water-soluble stabiliser, adjusting the measurements to your wrist size. Now proceed as for the necklace.

For the earrings, sew a large and a small circle for each one, as described above. For the small loops, sew short lines back and forth all around, always sewing into the blue silk. Join two circles together with two rows of rocaille beads; embroider with facetted beads and attach the earring findings.

Ice crystal

Stole and cuffs

A dreamily pretty stole with matching cuffs – this combination will definitely be your own unique creation. Presented here in stylish white, it is an ideal addition to your evening wardrobe. It would look equally good in other colours too.
The ends of the stole are made from flowers and leaves that are reminiscent of ice crystals. The centre piece is made from a hand-rolled silk shawl.

MATERIALS

Stole

- iron-on stabiliser, e.g. G 785 by Freudenberg in white, 80 × 90cm (31½ × 35½in)
- crêpe silk satin 08 in white, 80 × 90cm (31½ × 35½in)
- water-soluble stabiliser, e.g. Soluvlies by Freudenberg, 240 × 50cm (94½ × 19¾in)
- silk satin shawl, hand-rolled, 150 × 40cm (59 × 15¾in)
- spray adhesive
- sewing thread in black (for the bobbin)
- metallic embroidery thread in silver and black/silver

Cuffs

- silk satin, 80 × 45cm (31½in × 17¾in)
- iron-on stabiliser, e.g. G 785 by Freudenberg in white, 80 × 45cm (31½in × 17¾in)
- water-soluble stabiliser, e.g. Soluvlies by Freudenberg, 90 × 80cm (35½in × 31½in)
- spray adhesive
- sewing thread in black (for the bobbin)
- metallic embroidery thread in silver and black/silver
- 8 small press studs in white

INSTRUCTIONS

Stole

Iron white iron-on stabiliser to the reverse of the crêpe silk satin. This gives the silk stability and prevents it from fraying. The flowers and leaves for the ends are cut out from this silk.

Design freehand flowers and leaves or trace the patterns (see pages 24 and 25) using tracing paper. Make card templates of the motifs: one large and one small flower and one large and one small leaf. Transfer approx. twenty each of the large and small flowers and leaves on to the silk and cut out with sharp dressmaking scissors; the required number can be varied according to the formation, shape and size of the motifs. You will not know the exact number needed until you have laid them out.

Cut out four pieces, each 50 × 60cm (19¾ × 23½in), from water-soluble stabiliser; two of the pieces will form the base and two will act as the cover.

Shorten the silk shawl at each end by 15cm (6in). Lay approx. 8cm (3¼in) of each end on to a piece of stabiliser and secure with some spray adhesive. Spray the stabiliser pieces at each end of the shawl sparingly with adhesive and cover with the flowers and leaves. Lay the first flower pieces half on the end of the silk shawl and half on the water-soluble stabiliser. Make sure that the motifs always overlap a little at the points.

Once both ends of the shawl have been completely covered, spray again with spray adhesive. Place the second piece of stabiliser exactly on to each end and press down well. Leave the work for a short while, so that the fresh spray adhesive does not clog up the sewing needle.

Drop the feed dog on the sewing machine and attach the darning or freehand quilting foot. Use black thread on the bobbin, preferably spool embroidery thread, and metallic embroidery thread in silver for the top stitching. Now sew at high speed, but moving the work slowly. Edge the decorations in circular movements and sew the free areas in between in a radial or netting pattern. It is important to always sew at least one stitch into the edge of the neighbouring flower (as when darning), to avoid the seams falling apart later once the stabiliser has dissolved. The leaf shapes can be filled in with veins too.

Finally, sew some circles into the centres of the flowers using metallic embroidery thread in black/silver for the top stitching. Sew in a single line without interruption. To continue the line, sew along the outer edge of some of the leaves from one flower to the next, until all the inner areas are filled.

Once the sewing is complete, rinse the stabiliser in cold water. Leave the stole for a short while in the second rinsing water, so that the adhesive is completely dissolved too. When there is no more residue in the silk, roll up the stole in a large towel (do not wring) and then iron whilst damp.

Cuffs

For the cuffs, first reinforce the silk with the iron-on stabiliser as for the stole and cut out flowers and leaves following the pattern (see below).

The two cuffs should be made at the same time, side by side, so that both pieces look the same. Cut out the water-soluble stabiliser for both cuffs: two pieces measuring 45 × 40cm (17¾ × 15¾in) for each cuff. Spray with spray adhesive and cover with the silk decorations. Spray again sparingly with adhesive. Lay the covering stabiliser on top and press down.

Prepare and proceed with the sewing work in the same way as for the stole (see page 24).

Rinse out the stabiliser in cold water and iron while still damp. To fasten, sew four press studs on to each cuff with little stitches.

Coral reef

Top and necklace

This top and necklace are the perfect match. Let your imagination run riot – instead of floral decorations, geometric shapes can also be used. By using many different-sized motifs you can create a really vibrant look!

MATERIALS

Top

- crêpe silk satin 08 in white, 75 × 80cm (29½ × 31½in)
- silk paint in red, green and blue
- iron-on stabiliser, e.g. G 785 by Freudenberg in black, 75 × 80cm (29½ × 31½in)
- water-soluble stabiliser, e.g. Soluvlies by Freudenberg, 200 × 90cm (78¾ × 35½in)
- spray adhesive
- sewing thread in black, spool embroidery thread (for the bobbin)
- sewing thread in red
- metallic embroidery thread in red and turquoise
- glass beads in red, green, silver and black: approx. 15g (½oz) rocaille beads, approx. 8g (¼oz) bugle beads (7mm), approx. 39 facetted beads (diameter 4mm), approx. 20 facetted beads (diameter 6mm)
- beaded cord or silk cord, hand-rolled
- small chain fastenings or hooks and eyes

Necklace

- water-soluble stabiliser, e.g. Soluvlies by Freudenberg, approx. 80 × 80cm (31½ × 31½in)
- sewing thread in red
- metallic embroidery thread in red
- leather choker fastening in silver (karabiner hook)
- approx. 15g (½oz) rocaille beads and approx. 85 facetted beads (diameter 6mm) in red

INSTRUCTIONS

Top

Stretch the silk over the painting frame or clear plastic film and paint in various mixtures of red, green and blue/turquoise shades; the red shades should be dominant at the end. When painting, allow the edges to run, making a combination of shades.

Once dry, steam- or iron-fix the silk and finally rinse and iron. Reinforce the reverse side with black iron-on stabiliser.

Using sharp dressmaking scissors or the cutting wheel, cut out decorations freehand on the cutting mat or cut out motifs previously drawn on to the black iron-on stabiliser using a white watercolour pencil. Transfer the pattern for the top (see page 57) on to paper and cut out, adjusting the size if necessary (pattern = size 14). The design can now be sketched on to the pattern in some detail (see top of page 28). Try out the arrangement of silk motifs on top to see if the number needs adjusting.

Draw the pattern twice on water-soluble stabiliser using a graphite watercolour pencil, to make a base piece and a covering stabiliser. Add approx. 2cm (¾in) all round, as the work will pull in due to the number of seams. Draw on the darts, but do not cut out.

Cover the work surfaces. Lay down the first piece of stabiliser and spray sparingly with spray adhesive. Arrange the silk motifs on top and press down well. Spray everything again sparingly. Lay the covering stabiliser on top and press down.

Prior to sewing, drop the feed dog on the sewing machine and attach the darning foot or freehand quilting foot. Using black thread on the bobbin and red sewing thread for the top stitching, sew at high speed, but with slow turning movements.

Join up the silk motifs with lengthways and crossways stitches, as if darning. Catch the silk in with each seam, so that the seams will not come apart when the stabiliser is rinsed out later. Sew netting very carefully at the edges where there are no silk pieces and always join up the individual embroidery threads, to make a sturdy network. Leave out the darts when sewing. Using the metallic embroidery thread for top stitching, embroider over some of the decorations first with red and then with green lines.

Before stopping sewing, tack both darts, cut off the excess stabiliser and sew over in a netting pattern. Embroider small beads in various colours on to the completed top.

Check that all the silk edges have been attached and then rinse out the stabiliser in cold water, leaving for a short while in the final rinse water. Lay out to dry on a towel. Iron on the reverse beneath a towel.

Finally, attach a beaded cord (either shop bought or made yourself) or a rolled silk cord as a strap and sew on small chain fastenings or hooks and eyes at the back.

Necklace

The matching necklace is made of three layers of water-soluble stabiliser, each 40 × 35cm (15¾ × 13¾in), that form the base fabric for sewing when placed on top of one another. Work out the length of the necklace and draw it on to the top layer of stabiliser in the desired shape (oval or round).

Thread red sewing thread through a hand-sewing needle and, using little tacking stitches, sew all the lines of the necklace by hand, going through all three layers of the stabiliser and joining them together. You can use the photo on the right as a guide, in which thirteen hanging strands of approx. 3.5–7cm (1½–2¾in) were marked around the edge of the necklace and tacked on first.

Set up the sewing machine with red sewing thread for the top stitching and bobbin and attach the zigzag sewing foot. Sew the first seam over the tacking threads using small, narrow zigzag stitches; use straight stitch for the second. Use metallic embroidery thread as top stitching for the third seam, also using zigzag stitch.

Once the stabiliser has dissolved in cold water, leave the necklace to dry and then attach a fastening. Decorate the necklace with rocaille and facetted beads in red.

Tip

Using the same technique, you can also make multi-stranded necklaces. These are very effective when the individual strands are made in different colours. Metallic embroidery threads are available from retailers in many different colours.

Madrid

Necklace

Flowering twigs from nature were the inspiration for this fantastic filigree necklace.
It is just made from lengths of thread hung together and richly decorated with little glass beads.

Tip

Stability is important with this necklace, which is why the edges and links from one flower to another should be particularly carefully embroidered. Also, when rinsing out, a tiny amount of water-soluble stabiliser should be left in the piece.

MATERIALS

- water-soluble stabiliser, e.g. Soluvlies by Freudenberg, 70 × 90cm (27½ × 35½in)
- metallic embroidery thread in silver and red
- sewing thread in red and old rose
- glass beads in shades of red:
  approx. 20g (¾oz) rocaille beads,
  approx. 20 drop beads,
  approx. 15 disc beads,
  a few bugle and facetted beads
- jewellery fastenings, if required

INSTRUCTIONS

A sturdy base fabric is needed for this, which is why three layers of water-soluble stabiliser, each 45 × 35cm (17¾ × 13¾in), are used. Transfer the pattern (see page 58) on to the top layer of stabiliser. Hold the layers together with pins. Thread double metallic thread in silver through a hand-sewing needle and embroider around all the outlines of the flowers (apart from the small, red, marked leaves) using little backstitches. They form the framework for the piece.

For the first line of sewing, thread the sewing machine with red metallic thread for the top stitching and red sewing thread on the bobbin. For a line of sewing, start at one end and continue embroidering, without stopping, to the other end. Sew over the same lines several times.

Fill in all the flowers and leaves (including those marked in red) with embroidery stitches. Always work in a way that follows the shape, i.e. embroider a round shape using circular embroidery stitching. Form a network by joining the individual embroidery threads with round seams or by horizontal and vertical crossed lines of stitching. Include the metallic seams in silver stitched by hand into this and all further lines of sewing, i.e. sew a stitch from the centre of each flower over the metallic thread and then back to the centre.

For the first line of sewing, do not embroider the flowers too densely. They should look transparent. Oversew the links to the little free-hanging leaves several times. For the second line of sewing, use sewing thread in old rose for the top stitching and red for the bobbin and embroider over the red thread framework. This time though, leave out the small leaves marked in red, leaving them more transparent. Sew the third line using metallic thread in silver.

Rinse out the water-soluble stabiliser. Iron the necklace dry beneath a towel. Sew on the beads. Attach strands of beads in various lengths in the centre and at the ends. Sew on the fastening or make the strands of beads long enough that they can be loosely knotted to act as a fastening.

Eldorado

Necklace and brooch

This distinctive necklace made from metallic thread in gold and copper looks really expensive. It will look equally good as an attractive collar on a jumper or a dress. A matching brooch completes the look. Glass beads make the piece even more luxurious.

Tip

As the coloured areas narrow towards the top, it is better to start sewing in the centre of an area and fill in the areas to the right and left.

MATERIALS

- water-soluble stabiliser, e.g. Soluvlies by Freudenberg, 80 × 80cm (31½ × 31½in)
- metallic embroidery thread in gold and copper
- 32 rocaille beads and 96 facetted beads (diameter 4mm) in copper, 96 pyramid beads in gold (for a total of 32 strands of beads around the necklace)
- brooch, triangular, three-piece (frame, centre-piece, back with pin)

INSTRUCTIONS

Necklace

The base used during the sewing of the necklace is formed from three layers of water-soluble stabiliser laid on top of one another. Transfer the pattern (see page 57) to the top layer of stabiliser. Thread a hand-sewing needle with metallic embroidery thread in gold and sew all the lines of the necklace through the three layers of stabiliser with small tacking stitches.

Set up the sewing machine using gold metallic embroidery thread in the bobbin for all the sewing. Using metallic thread in gold for the top stitching, sew the pre-drawn lines or the tacking lines with little stitches in circles close together. Then as with darning, fill the areas with dense lengthways lines (alternating between gold and copper). Keep catching the edge with a stitch and then turn the work and sew back over it.

As a fastening, sew a loop to one end of the necklace with small, close zigzag stitches; attach a bead to the other end. If necessary, correct any gaps and then rinse out the stabiliser in cold water and iron the work beneath a towel. Finally, attach strands of beads as in the photo.

Brooch

Place the centre of the brooch on to three layers of water-soluble stabiliser, then draw around it approx. 1cm (½in) larger. Position the coloured areas to match the necklace (see photo). To make the brooch, work in the same way as for the necklace. Embroider the seams very closely together to form the covering for the centre of the brooch. Stretch the shape tightly over the centre-piece and sew together across on the back. Press the work into the frame and place the back with pin on top. Fold over the metal flaps of the frame and press down firmly.

Silver moon

Flower pins and bag

These accessories would be great for a summer's night party: two flowers at the neckline and a handbag with a matching decorative flower.

MATERIALS

Flower pins

- water-soluble stabiliser, e.g. Soluvlies by Freudenberg, 40 × 40cm (15¾ × 15¾in)
- spray adhesive
- lamé crochet thread in silver (remnant)
- sewing thread in blue
- metallic embroidery thread in silver
- silver wire, diameter 0.25mm, approx. 1.5m (59in) long
- glass beads in shades of blue and turquoise: approx. 5g (¼oz) rocaille beads, approx. 8g (¼oz) bugle beads, approx. 6 facetted beads (diameter 6mm), approx. 7 round beads (diameter 10mm)
- chiffon in blue (remnant)
- 2 brooch pins

Bag

- water-soluble stabiliser, e.g. Soluvlies by Freudenberg, 100 × 60cm (39¼ × 23½in)
- spray adhesive
- lamé crochet thread in silver, 25g (1oz)
- chiffon in blue, 120 × 60cm (47¼ × 23½in)
- metallic embroidery thread in silver
- iron-on stabiliser, e.g. S 320 by Freudenberg, 3.5 × 22cm (1½ × 8¾in)
- bag clasp (small chain)
- chiffon in blue and turquoise (remnants)
- silver wire, diameter 0.25mm, approx. 70cm (27½in) long
- 3 round beads (diameter 10mm), 2 facetted beads (diameter 10mm) in blue
- safety pin (optional)

INSTRUCTIONS

Flower pins

For both flower pins, draw the petal shapes on to the top of two layers of water-soluble stabiliser (number depends upon desired size). Design them freehand or transfer the patterns (see below).

Thread the silver lamé yarn through a darning needle with a large eye and sew through both layers of stabiliser, edging the individual petal shapes with embroidery stitches and marking some veins. These now form the framework for sewing (see top of page 36).

Set up the sewing machine with blue sewing thread on the bobbin and metallic embroidery thread for the top stitching. Drop the feed dog and attach the darning or freehand quilting foot. Embroider the petals with curves and straight lines. Avoid sewing the lines too close together. Embroider again on the reverse side. This helps the sewing thread to stay in place and the petals are embroidered in blue and silver on both sides. When embroidering, make sure that every line of hand-worked embroidery around the edge of the petals is caught with a sewing machine stitch (see top of page 36).

To assemble the flowers, cut up five silver wires each approx. 12cm (4¾in) long. Thread on a bead and twist the wire in half. Bind all five wires together with a piece of chiffon and silver wire. Using metallic embroidery thread, sew the petals underneath the bead on to the 'chiffon stem' – first the small ones, then the large shapes. Decorate the flowers by sewing on beads or strands of beads. Sew a brooch pin on to each flower.

Bag

Draw the pattern for the bag (see page 59) on to two layers of water-soluble stabiliser, each 40 × 50cm (15¾ × 19¾in). Cover the work surface, lay out the first layer of stabiliser and spray sparingly with spray adhesive. Cover the whole area of the bag with lamé yarn in silver, taking care not to go over the edges of the pattern. Spray with spray adhesive and cover with the second layer of stabiliser. Press down.

Cut out two layers of chiffon each 40 × 50cm (15¾ × 19¾in), spray each layer with a little spray adhesive and press one after the other down on to the stabiliser, without creasing.

Set up the sewing machine with metallic embroidery thread in silver for both the top stitching and the bobbin. Attach the sewing foot for straight stitching. The sewing is done on the stabiliser side; first mark the outline of the bag, then sew over the whole shape to join the lamé thread firmly to the chiffon.

After sewing, rinse out the stabiliser in cold water, leaving to soak for a little while in the rinsing water, so that the adhesive and the stabiliser are completely dissolved. Iron the piece for the bag dry beneath a towel.

Cut out the bag shape, fold in half and attach a strip of iron-on stabiliser 3.5 × 22cm (1½ × 8¾in) to the fold line to form the bottom of the bag. Sew up the side seams approx. 10cm (4in) and sew diagonally across the corners at the bottom of the bag. Using metallic embroidery thread, sew the top pieces to the bag clasp through the pre-punched holes.

For the flowers, cut out five large and four smaller shapes from the chiffon remnants according to the pattern (see bottom of page 34). Lay out some water-soluble stabiliser, spray with adhesive, place the chiffon shapes on top, spray again with adhesive and cover with a second layer of stabiliser.

The chiffon flowers are basically made in the same way as for the flower pins (see sewing sample above). Set up the sewing machine with metallic embroidery thread in silver for the top and bobbin thread. Lower the feed dog and embroider the chiffon petals using the darning or freehand quilting foot. Edge with small circular movements and fill the centre with straight lines for the veins. Sew at high speed, whilst guiding by hand with slow turning movements. Finally, rinse out the stabiliser and iron the petals dry beneath a towel.

To make up the flowers, cut up five silver wires each approx. 12cm (4¾in) long. Thread on a bead and twist the wire in half. Bind all five wires together with a piece of chiffon and silver wire. Using metallic embroidery thread, sew the petals underneath the bead on to the 'chiffon stem'. Sew the complete flower to the bag or attach from inside using a safety pin.

Red roses

Jewellery set

This jewellery set has a lovely lightness and transparency to it. It looks both delicate and luxurious at the same time. Very few materials are needed to make this distinct necklace with matching earrings and bracelet, as only remnants of silk or tulle are required.

> **Tip**
> Always allow for twice as much water-soluble stabiliser, since you will need both a base piece and a piece the same size to cover it with.

MATERIALS

- water-soluble stabiliser, e.g. Soluvlies by Freudenberg, approx. 120 × 90cm (47¼ × 35½in)
- silk or tulle in red
- spray adhesive
- sewing thread in red (for the bobbin)
- metallic embroidery thread in red (for the top stitching)
- approx. 200 glass facetted beads in red, diameter 6mm
- 2 earring findings in silver

INSTRUCTIONS

Necklace

Following the design, transfer the pattern for the necklace (see page 56) to scale on to paper and cut out. Draw approx. 160 circles – diameter 1–1.5cm (approx. ½in) inside the shape of the necklace for the flowers. Leave a gap in the centre for your neck. Cut out the centre shape and check to see whether your head will fit through the neck opening, as the necklace has no fastening.

Cut out the necklace shape twice from stabiliser, leaving a 2cm (¾in) margin around the outside. Using a graphite watercolour pencil, transfer the circles for the flowers on to one of the pieces of stabiliser. Cut out circles from red silk or a remnant of tulle to act as a base for the flowers.

Spray the base piece of stabiliser sparingly with spray adhesive and cover with the flower shapes according to the pattern, pressing down well. Spray again with a little spray adhesive and cover with the second layer of stabiliser.

When sewing, use sewing thread in red for the bobbin and metallic embroidery thread in red for the top stitching. Sew at high speed with a darning or freehand quilting foot, while making slow turning movements. First sew the flowers in circular movements, then make connecting lines, as when darning, always working from the middle outwards. Always sew two to three stitches out over the red base fabric, so that small loops are formed at the edge. This gives the flowers greater transparency.

Tip

A really lacy necklace can be made without using lace or silk. Embroider the flower shapes directly on to the water-soluble stabiliser. However, you must use at least three layers of stabiliser as the support material.

After finishing each flower, sew a bridge to the next one. Do this by making two lines of straight stitch on top of one another and sew a third line over the top using a narrow zigzag stitch.

Rinse out the sewing in cold water and lay to dry on a towel.

Sew on the beads using metallic embroidery thread. Always stitch two to three times through the bead and sew the thread through the bridge to the next flower.

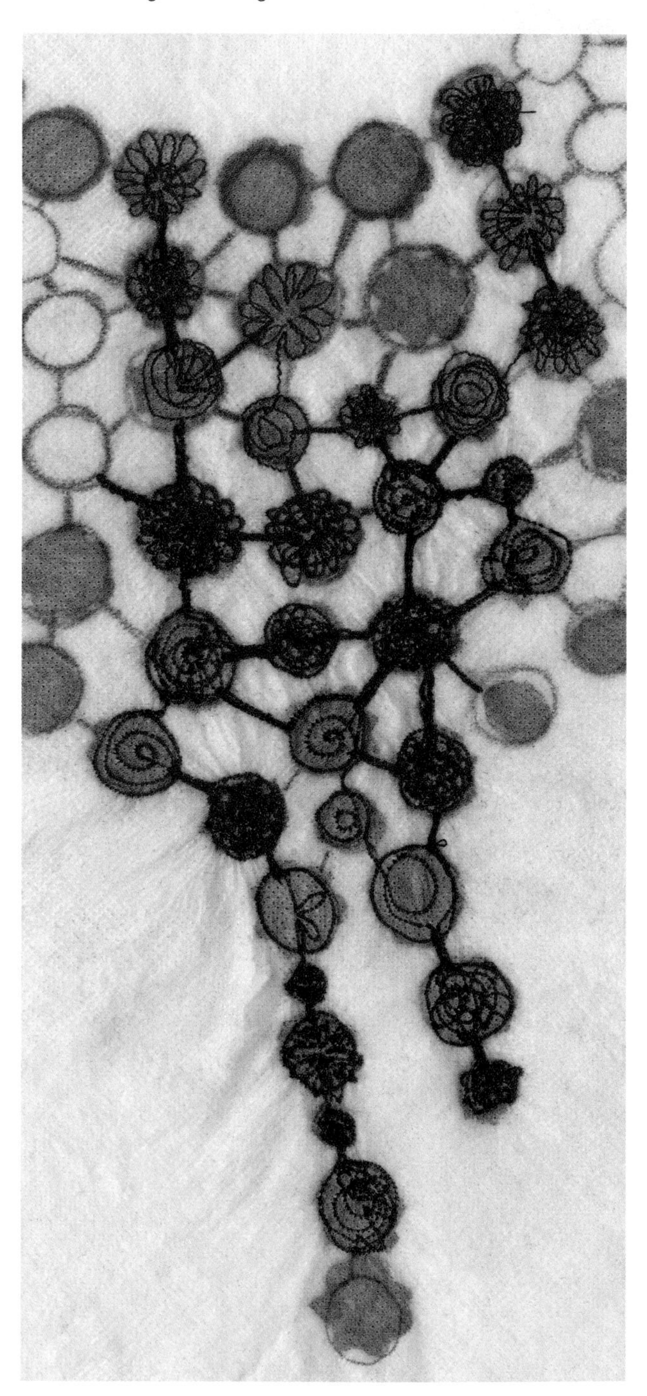

Earrings

The earrings are made using the same principle as for the necklace.

Draw a design for the earrings on paper and then transfer twice on to water-soluble stabiliser using a graphite watercolour pencil. Each earring is made up of four circles with a diameter of 1–2cm (approx ½–¾in) and an oval approx. 2.5cm (1in) made from silk or tulle.

For this lace work, place another layer of water-soluble stabiliser for stability underneath. Avoid cutting the stabiliser too small, i.e. leave at least 3–4cm (1¼–1½in) around the edge, so that the work can be moved more easily when sewing.

Rinse out the piece in cold water and dry on a towel. Embroider the earrings on both sides with beads, as they will dangle freely. Finally, attach an earring finding to the top of the first flower of each one.

Bracelet

Make the bracelet in the same way as for the necklace. Draw the bracelet once on to paper and then transfer it on to the water-soluble stabiliser using a graphite watercolour pencil, with two circles of approx. 2cm (¾in) in diameter in each row. Adjust the number of rows according to the size of your wrist. At one end, draw a double loop and at the other a single one.

When sewing, ensure that the edging is secure by sewing several times over the outer edge using straight stitch and zigzag stitch; at the same time, catch in the individual flowers and also the loops.

Sew a bead on to the single loop, push the double loop through the loop with the bead and pull back over the bead to fasten the bracelet.

Tip

As an alternative to sewing on beads, colour-matched gemstones can be stuck on using gemstone adhesive.

Green eyes

Necklace and bracelet

This green set is made with a few silk remnants and a lot of pleasure. The beads and silk are in matching shades, making this jewellery set really attractive.
We recommend that you make both pieces together on one piece of water-soluble stabiliser, saving both time and material.

MATERIALS

- water-soluble stabiliser, e.g. Soluvlies by Freudenberg, approx. 50 × 80cm (19¾ × 31½in)
- some green silk
- spray adhesive
- some iron-on stabiliser, e.g. G 785 by Freudenberg in black
- sewing thread in green (for the bobbin)
- metallic embroidery thread in green (for the top stitching)
- glass beads in green, for the necklace: 49 disc beads, 24 large facetted beads, 106 small facetted beads, 23 drop beads and approx. 15g (½oz) rocaille beads; for the bracelet: 16 disc beads, 9 large facetted beads, 31 small facetted beads and 16 rocaille beads

INSTRUCTIONS

Necklace

Cut out two pieces of water-soluble stabiliser 30 × 40cm (11¾ × 15¾in). On one piece of stabiliser, draw the outline of the necklace freehand or following the template (see page 59).

Reinforce the green silk remnants with iron-on stabiliser in black. Using a white watercolour pencil, draw eight each of the small, medium and large drops and 23 clover leaves (see template left) on to the black side and cut out.

Lay out the piece of stabiliser with the pre-drawn side face down, spray with adhesive and arrange the motifs with the green side down. Arrange the drops so that they become smaller towards the fastening at the back. Spray sparingly with spray adhesive, cover with a layer of stabiliser and press down firmly.

Turn the work over for sewing. The pre-drawn side of the stabiliser is then uppermost, with the green silk decorations and pre-drawn bridges clearly visible. Do not sew over the edge of the silk decorations. The bridges are made from three lines sewn on top of one another using straight stitch. Sew the loops on the necklace straight into each end and make them sturdy using a small zigzag stitch.

Rinse out the piece in cold water and iron dry beneath a towel. Attach the beads as in the photo or any way you like. A disc bead on one end and the loop on the other end form the fastening.

Bracelet

The bracelet is made in the same way as the necklace using two pieces of stabiliser approx. 20 × 30cm (7¾ × 11¾in; template on page 59). Sew a large facetted bead to the short loop. To close, pull the double loop through the opening under this bead and hook over the bead.

Florence

Belt and bag

This white silk satin belt and handbag set with black decoration is especially eye-catching. The belt fastens with hooks and eyes; a kilt pin could also be used.

Tip
The work should always be left for a while before sewing, so that the fresh spray adhesive does not clog up the needle.

MATERIALS

Belt

- silk satin 08 in white, 110 × 50cm (43¼ × 19¾in), in black, 90 × 20cm (35½ × 7¾in)
- iron-on stabiliser, e.g. G 785 by Freudenberg in white, 110 × 50cm (43¼ × 19¾in), in black, 90 × 20cm (35½ × 7¾in)
- water-soluble stabiliser, e.g. Soluvlies by Freudenberg, approx. 130 × 60cm (51¼ × 23½in)
- spray adhesive
- metallic embroidery thread in silver
- sewing thread in black
- 2 pairs of hooks and eyes

Bag

- silk satin 08 in white, 60 × 40cm (23½ × 15¾in), in black, approx. 90 × 60cm (35½ × 23½in)
- iron-on stabiliser, e.g. G 785 by Freudenberg in white, 60 × 40cm (23½ × 15¾in), in black, 90 × 60cm (35½ × 23½in)
- water-soluble stabiliser, e.g. Soluvlies by Freudenberg, 50 × 80cm (19¾ × 31½in)
- spray adhesive
- iron-on stabiliser, e.g. S 320 by Freudenberg, approx. 70 × 40cm (27½ × 15¾in)
- metallic embroidery thread in silver
- sewing thread in black
- 1 pair of bag handles (with karabiner hooks and D-rings)

INSTRUCTIONS

Belt

For the decoration on the belt, reinforce the black silk with black iron-on stabiliser, to make it sturdy and to prevent the decoration from fraying when cut out.

Trace both patterns for the decoration (see page 46) and prepare a template for each on firm card. Draw eighteen long and fourteen round decorations on to the stabiliser side using a white watercolour pencil and cut out using sharp dressmaking scissors. Make sure that you have both right and left decorations for the design; transfer the mirror image for the other half of the decoration by simply turning the template over.

For the belt, reinforce 110 × 50cm (43¼ × 19¾in) of white silk satin with white iron-on stabiliser. Draw the pattern for the belt (see page 59) to scale using a graphite watercolour pencil on the front side, then arrange the decorations on top and draw around them. Cut out the rounded edges of the decorations at the outside edge of the silk according to the pattern.

Transfer the pattern twice to water-soluble stabiliser and cut around, leaving a margin. Cover the work surface and spread out a piece of stabiliser; spray sparingly with spray adhesive and lay the white, cut-out piece for the belt on top. Spray again with a little adhesive over the pre-drawn pattern; arrange the black silk decorations according to the pattern and press down. Spray again with adhesive, cover with the second piece of stabiliser and press down well.

Set up the sewing machine: use metallic embroidery thread in silver for the top stitching and black sewing thread for the bobbin. Attach the sewing foot for zigzag stitch.

A variation that does not require water-soluble stabiliser is the appliqué method: double-sided adhesive stabiliser is ironed on to the reverse side of the black silk satin. Place the templates on to the paper side of the stabiliser, draw around the edges and cut out the decorations. Remove the backing paper and place the coated side on to the reinforced belt according to the pattern. Lay a damp towel over the top and iron on. Continue as before. This appliqué method using adhesive stabiliser is also used for the items on pages 52–55.

Either use an embroidery stitch or a simple zigzag stitch to edge the individual decorations. Sew precisely around the outside edges and make sure that the stitching is sewn as steadily as possible, so that there are no gaps.

After sewing, rinse out the water-soluble stabiliser. Leave to soak for a while in the final rinse water. If too much spray adhesive was applied and it is still sticking to the silk, add some fabric softener or a few dessert spoons of vinegar to the rinse water. Roll up in a towel and then iron dry beneath another towel. Sew the hooks and eyes on to the belt.

Tip

The elegant effect of this belt and bag comes from the strong contrast of colours. You can also combine other colours effectively with either white or black, e.g. burgundy and white or pink and black.

Bag

For the decorations on the bag, reinforce the black silk with black iron-on stabiliser, e.g. G 785 by Freudenberg.

Trace both the patterns for the decorations (see page 46) and prepare a template for each on firm card. Draw sixteen long and six round decorations on to the stabiliser side using a white watercolour pencil and cut out. Make sure that you have both right and left decorations for the design by transferring the mirror image for the other half of the decoration.

Both halves of the bag are made in one piece. Reinforce the white silk satin 50 × 40cm (19¾ × 15¾in) with the white iron-on stabiliser, e.g. G 785 by Freudenberg. Transfer the pattern (see page 59) twice to water-soluble stabiliser 50 × 40cm (19¾ × 15¾in); cover and sew following the instructions for the belt.

After sewing, rinse out the stabiliser. Leave to soak for a while in the final rinse water. If the silk is still sticky, add some fabric softener or some vinegar to the rinse water. Roll up in a towel and then iron dry beneath another towel.

Reinforce the piece for the bag with 48 × 38cm (19 × 15in) of iron-on stabiliser, e.g. S 320 by Freudenberg. Fold in half, right sides together, close up the side seams and sew a 6cm (2¼in) line of stitching across the corners on each side (see pattern, page 59) to make the bottom of the bag.

For the lining, cut out a piece of black silk satin 48 × 38cm (19 × 15in); close up the side seams as for the bag and sew across the corners. Place the bag and the lining pieces together incorporating two loops of 4 × 2cm (1½ × ¾in) at the top as in the pattern diagram and pin together, after threading through the D-rings for the bag handles.

Cut out two strips, each 8 × 38cm (3¼ × 15in) from black silk satin, fold in half, iron and reinforce each one with a strip of iron-on stabiliser, e.g. S 320 by Freudenberg. Sew the strips to the top edges of the bag pieces, incorporating the loops with the D-rings. Hook the bag handles on to the D-rings using the karabiner hooks.

Indian summer

Top and bracelet

The unique woven design of this set makes it really attractive. And it is all possible with the help of water-soluble stabiliser.
With very few materials and a lot of creativity, you can devise beautiful textile surfaces. Warm, strong colours have been used for this top with matching bracelet.

Tip

If the silk is still sticky after rinsing, then too much spray adhesive has been used. Just put some fabric softener or a few dessertspoons of vinegar into the rinsing water.

MATERIALS

- silk satin in white, approx. 75 × 110cm (29½ × 43¼in)
- silk paint in yellow, orange and brown
- iron-on stabiliser, e.g. G 785 by Freudenberg in skin tone, 75 × 110cm (29½ × 43¼in)
- water-soluble stabiliser, e.g. Soluvlies by Freudenberg, 190 × 90cm (74¾ × 35½in)
- spray adhesive
- sewing thread in black, spool embroidery thread (for the bobbin)
- metallic embroidery thread in gold and copper
- approx. 25g (1oz) rocaille beads and approx. 10g (¼oz) bugle beads (7mm) in both gold and copper, approx. 50 facetted beads (diameter 4mm) in gold
- 6 pairs of hooks and eyes (for the back and neck fastenings)

INSTRUCTIONS

Top

Stretch the silk over the painting frame or clear plastic film and paint wet-in-wet with the silk paints (see 'Painting silk', page 10). Dampen the silk and starting with yellow, make pretty colour runs through to dark brown. Leave to dry, steam- or iron-fix the silk and finally, reinforce with iron-on stabiliser to make the silk sturdy and to prevent it from fraying when cutting out the decorations.

Draw lots of different shapes on the stabiliser side of the painted silk in various sizes, e.g. natural shapes like leaves and twigs, and cut out. Work freehand or transfer the patterns (see page 51) and make templates too if you want. This top will look very natural if the design is random. Lay the motifs on to the pattern to see if you have the required number of decorations. Any excess can be used for the bracelet.

Transfer the pattern for the top (see page 59) to scale on to paper, adjust as necessary depending on the size (pattern = size 14). Using a watercolour pencil, transfer the pattern to water-soluble stabiliser. Add approx. 1.5–2cm (½–¾in) around the outside edges, as the whole piece will get smaller when sewn. Draw on the darts and generously cut out the whole pattern twice, leaving a margin of 2–3cm (¾–1¼) in all around.

Cover the work surfaces with paper, lay out a piece of stabiliser and spray sparingly with spray adhesive. Arrange the cut-out silk motifs with the silk side uppermost on to the water-soluble stabiliser. Make sure that the motifs touch and overlap a little at the corners. Finally, press down well. Spray again sparingly with spray adhesive, lay the covering stabiliser on top, without creasing, and press down.

Before starting sewing, drop the feed dog on the sewing machine and attach the darning or freehand quilting foot. Use black sewing thread for the bobbin thread on the sewing machine; for the top stitching, first use metallic embroidery thread in gold and, when sewing for the second time, use copper. When sewing the first time, all the motifs are secured; when sewing the second time, embroider the cross lines for the netting and embroidery lines on the leaves.

With this transparent weave, you have to be very careful that every line of stitching catches the silk and that there are no gaps. Sew the free areas first lengthways and then crossways, as when darning, to form the netting. Finally, sew around the outside edges with zigzag stitch. Check all the seams again to ensure that there are no loose bits.

Rinse out the work in cold water and leave to soak in the final rinse water for a while, so that the stabiliser and spray adhesive dissolve without any residue. Roll up in a towel (do not wring) and finally iron dry beneath another towel.

After drying, start the lacy work with the bead embroidery. For the top, rocaille beads are embroidered close together on to some of the netting threads. Slip several beads on to the thread, place over a netting seam, pull the thread through the silk and then sew behind each bead around the netting thread. Bugle beads and small facetted beads decorate some of the flowers and leaves. The number is down to personal taste.

For the rear fastening, sew a strip of silk to both ends of the back of the top approx. 20 × 6cm (7¾ × 2¼in), fold in half inwards and secure by hand. Attach hooks and eyes as a fastening.

Try on to see where the hooks and eyes (two pairs) will need to go for the neck fastening.

Bracelet

For the bracelet, measure your wrist in advance and also decide on the width. Draw the outline of the bracelet, including the fastening loops. You may need to add more fastening loops depending on the width. The bracelet shown is 5.5cm (2¼in) wide and is fastened with three loops and three corresponding beads. Cut out the silk motifs a little smaller this time and make the netting areas in between much narrower.

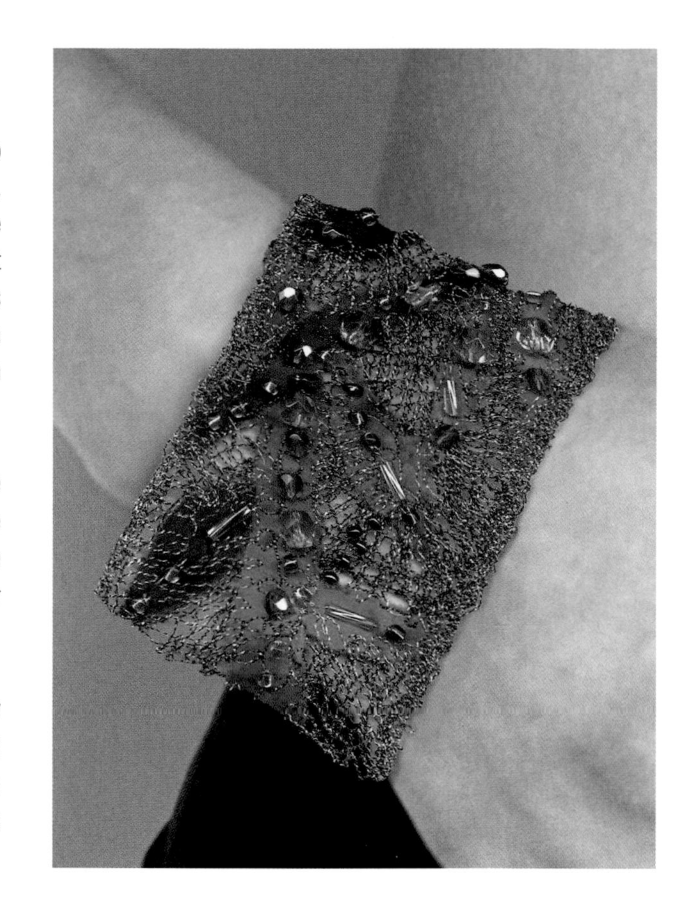

Work in the same way as for the top. Avoid cutting the water-soluble stabiliser too closely for such tiny work; leave at least 5cm (2in) extra all round, so that it can easily be moved when sewing and if necessary place another layer underneath before sewing.

Take special care when sewing around the edge; sew around it several times – a few times in straight stitch and twice using zigzag stitch, always catching in the motifs in the centre, so that the bracelet is sturdy. The loops are sewn in at the same time too.

Rinse in cold water, iron dry beneath a towel, sew on the beads and attach the fastening beads.

Marrakech

Stole and cap

A silk shawl in old rose forms the basis of this very feminine look with a touch of the orient. The paisley appliqué and beaded fringes make it a really glamorous accessory. The chic silk cap complements the stole perfectly.

Tip

If you want to make both pieces match, you should measure and paint the silk for both items together, so that the shades for the stole and cap are the same.

MATERIALS

Stole

- silk satin 08 in white, approx. 90 × 60cm (35½ × 23½in)
- silk paint in old rose and Bordeaux
- double-sided adhesive stabiliser, e.g. Vliesofix Freudenberg, approx. 90 × 60cm (35½ × 23½in)
- chiffon shawl in old rose, 180 × 50cm (70¾ × 19¾in)
- water-soluble stabiliser, e.g. Soluvlies by Freudenberg, 180 × 100cm (70¾ × 39¼in)
- spray adhesive
- metallic embroidery thread in silver
- approx. 40g (1½oz) rocaille beads in old rose, approx. 12g (½oz) bugle beads (7mm), 60 disc and 60 pyramid beads in red

Cap

- silk satin 08 in white, approx. 50 × 80cm (19¾ × 31½in)
- silk paint in old rose and Bordeaux
- iron-on stabiliser, e.g. S 320 by Freudenberg, approx. 90 × 40cm (35½ × 15¾in)
- metallic embroidery thread in silver
- double-sided adhesive stabiliser, e.g. Vliesofix by Freudenberg, approx. 30 × 60cm (11¾ × 23½in)

INSTRUCTIONS

Stole

Paint half the white silk satin wet-in-wet (see page 10) in old rose, then mix some Bordeaux into the old rose and paint the other half with this shade. Leave to dry and then steam- or iron-fix.

Place double-sided adhesive stabiliser with the rough (coated) side to the reverse side of the painted silk satin and iron dry for three to four seconds. Trace the patterns for the paisley decorations (see page 54) and make templates from firm card. Draw around ten to twelve motifs in all sizes on to the paper side of the adhesive stabiliser and cut out.

Spread out the chiffon shawl over a surface suitable for ironing and cover each end for about 50cm (19¾in) with the cut-out silk motifs. Remove the backing paper from the silk motifs and place coated side down; cover with a damp towel and iron lightly for eight to ten seconds.

Cut out the water-soluble stabiliser twice in the size of the chiffon shawl. Spread out one piece of stabiliser. Spray very sparingly with spray adhesive and lay the shawl on top without creasing. Spray again with some adhesive. Cover with the second piece of stabiliser and press down firmly. Draw the outlines of the smallest template approximately ten times on to the piece of stabiliser on top of the design using the graphite watercolour pencil. These motifs are patterns to be embroidered later. They are embroidered with just metallic embroidery thread in silver, without using silk decorations (see page 54, top left).

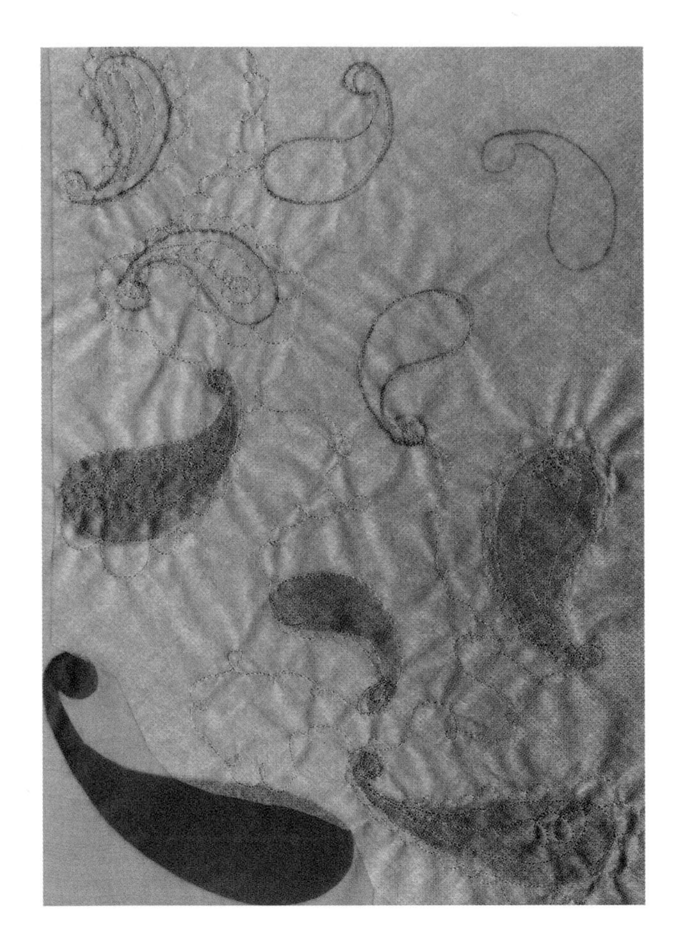

Sew approx. 30 strings of beads on to each end of the shawl. Make them by working with one thread at a time: thread on three rocaille beads in old rose, five times with a bugle bead in between each group. Finish off by stringing on a disc bead, a pyramid bead and a rocaille bead and pass the thread back through all the beads. Secure the thread in the seam and go on to the next string.

Set up the sewing machine: use metallic embroidery thread in silver for both the bobbin and top thread, attach the darning foot or freehand quilting foot and drop the feed dog. Starting at the lower edge, fill in the motifs with embroidery, edge them with a loop design and link them to the next motif. Sew at high speed, but turn the work slowly by hand and do not pull.

Once all the silk motifs are filled in, embroider the pre-drawn motifs too. The centre piece of the chiffon shawl should be kept plain.

Wash out the stole in cold water, rinse and roll up in a large towel; iron while still damp.

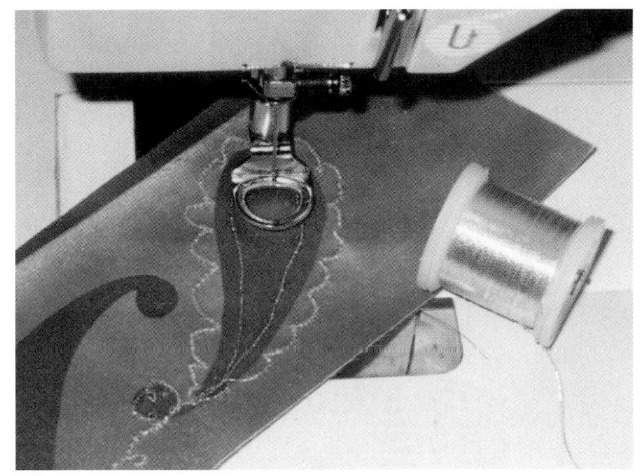

Cap

Paint up to three quarters of the silk satin wet-in-wet (see page 10) in old rose . Mix in some Bordeaux and paint the rest with the darker shade. Leave to dry and steam- or iron-fix.

Iron the darker silk on to 25 × 25cm (9¾ × 9¾in) pieces of iron-on stabiliser on both sides. Transfer the pattern (see page 59) for the cap; the circle for the top of the cap has a diameter of 21cm (8¼in). To give the cap shape, make the four darts as shown on the pattern. Embroider a loop design on the top of the cap using metallic embroidery thread in silver.

For the edge of the cap – 59cm (23¼in) long, 6cm (2¼in) high – reinforce the silk in the lighter shade with a strip of iron-on stabiliser of the same length.

Place double-sided adhesive stabiliser with the rough side to the wrong side of the dark painted silk satin and iron on dry for three to four seconds. Choose a decoration as a pattern (for the cap the motifs should all be the same size) and transfer eight times to the paper side of the adhesive stabiliser; cut out.

Iron on and embroider the motifs around the edge of the cap as shown for the stole. Make the edge of the cap into a ring, close up the seam; cut in around the top of the cap approx. 0.5cm (¼in) and sew both pieces together. Iron another strip of silk approx. 6cm (2¼in) wide to the inside of the edge.

Tip

If you want to make a matching bag, use the 'Florence' model as a pattern and apply paisley motifs instead of the ones used there.

Patterns

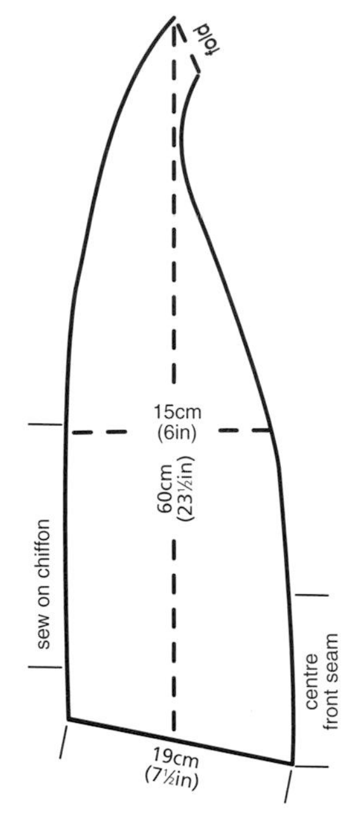

Halter-neck top, page 16

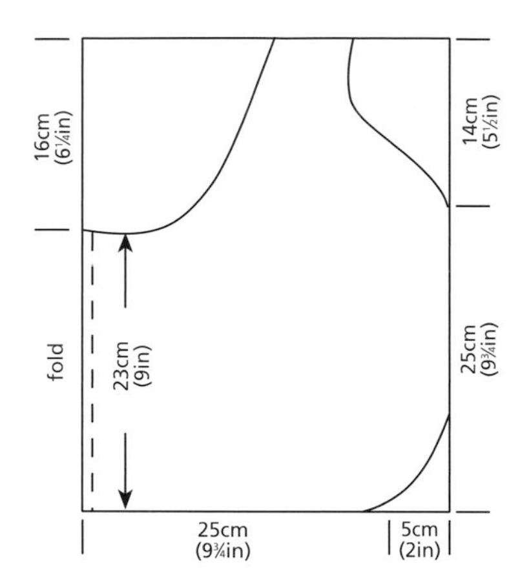

Decorative collar, page 12

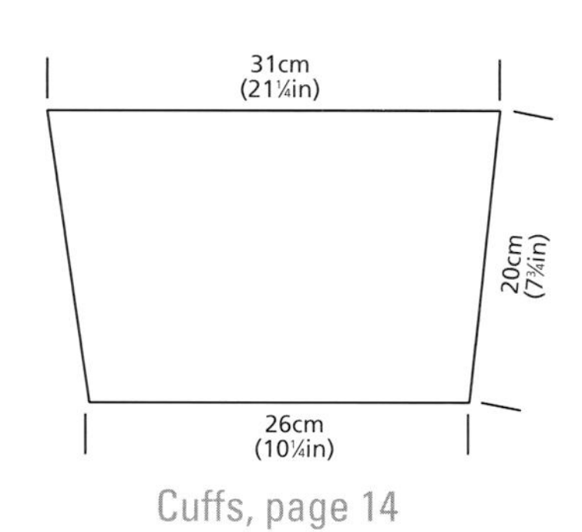

Cuffs, page 14

47cm
(18½in)
48cm
(19in)
68cm
(26¾in)
30cm
(11¾in)
30cm
(11¾in)
27cm
(10¾in)

Necklace, page 38

Halter-neck top, page 16

Enlarge by 200% using a photocopier.

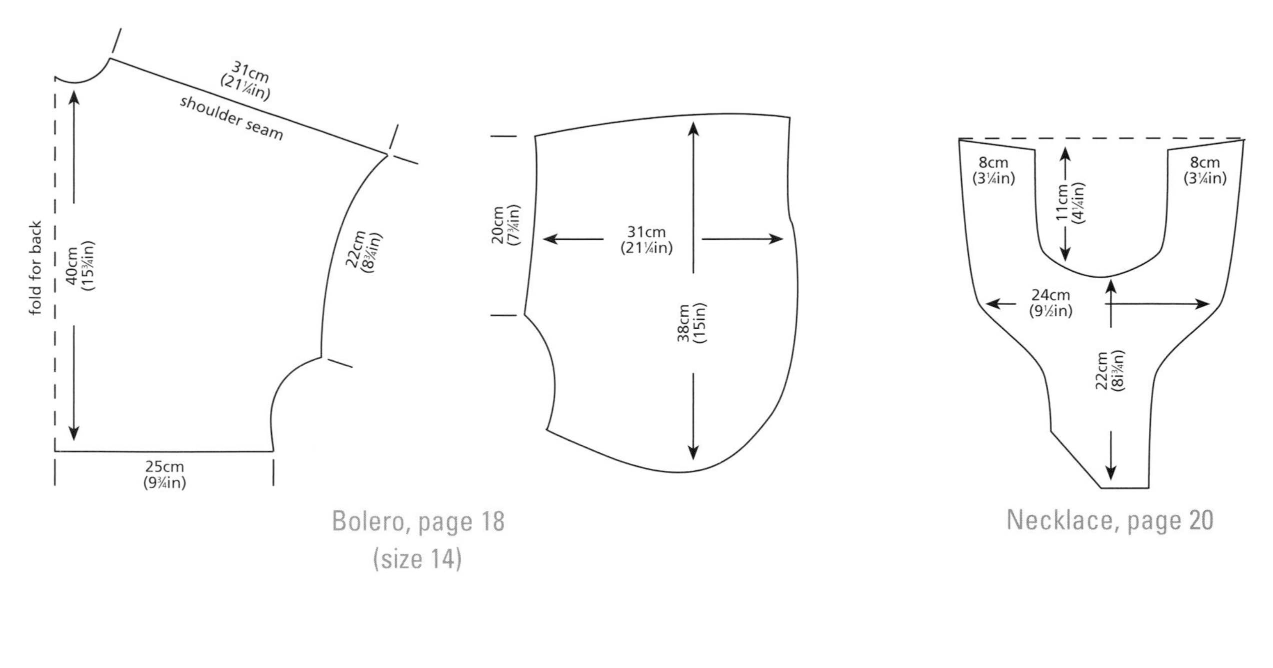

Bolero, page 18
(size 14)

Necklace, page 20

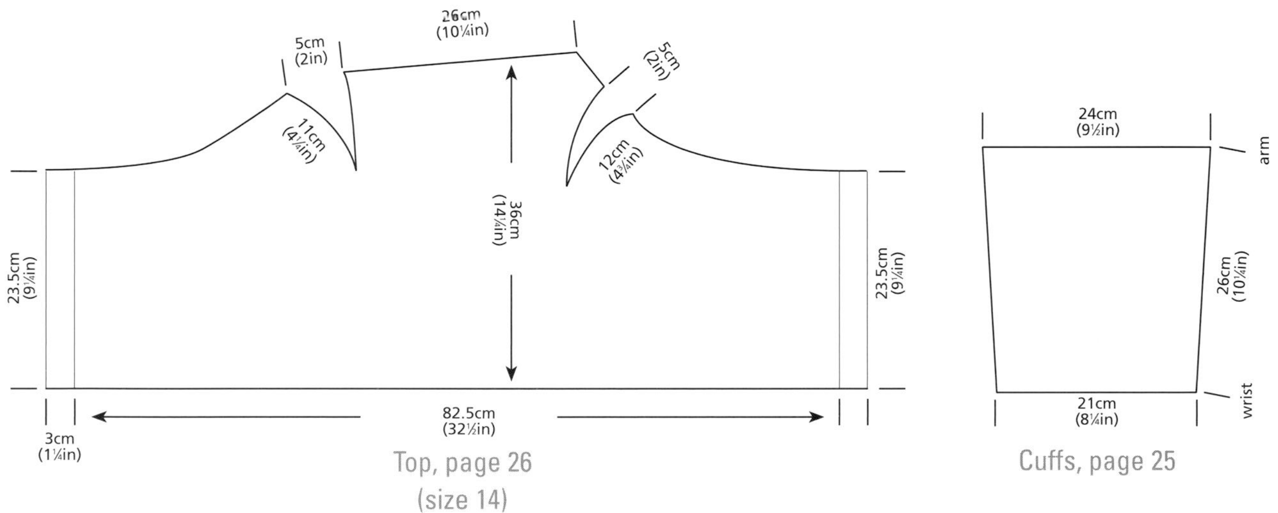

Top, page 26
(size 14)

Cuffs, page 25

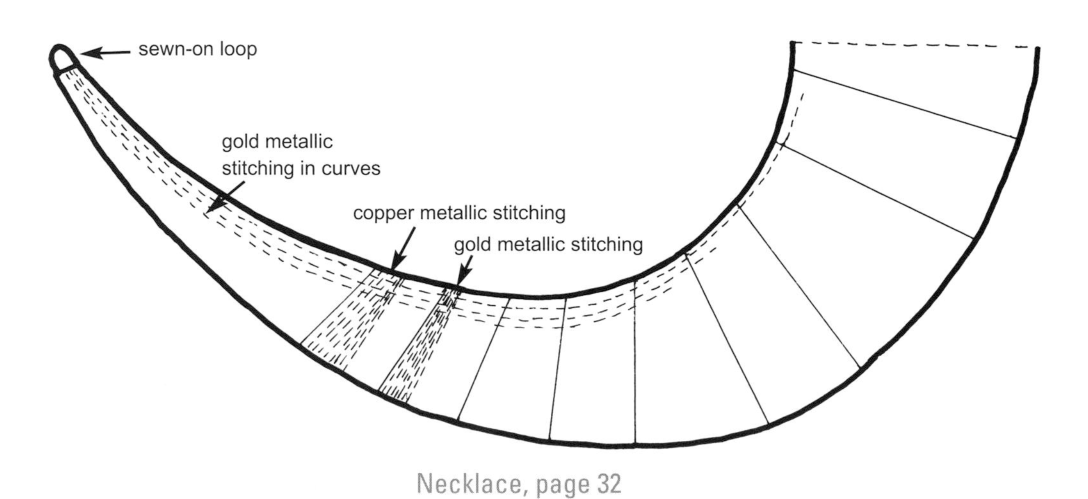

Necklace, page 32

Enlarge by 200% using a photocopier.

Necklace, page 30

Enlarge by 200% using a photocopier.

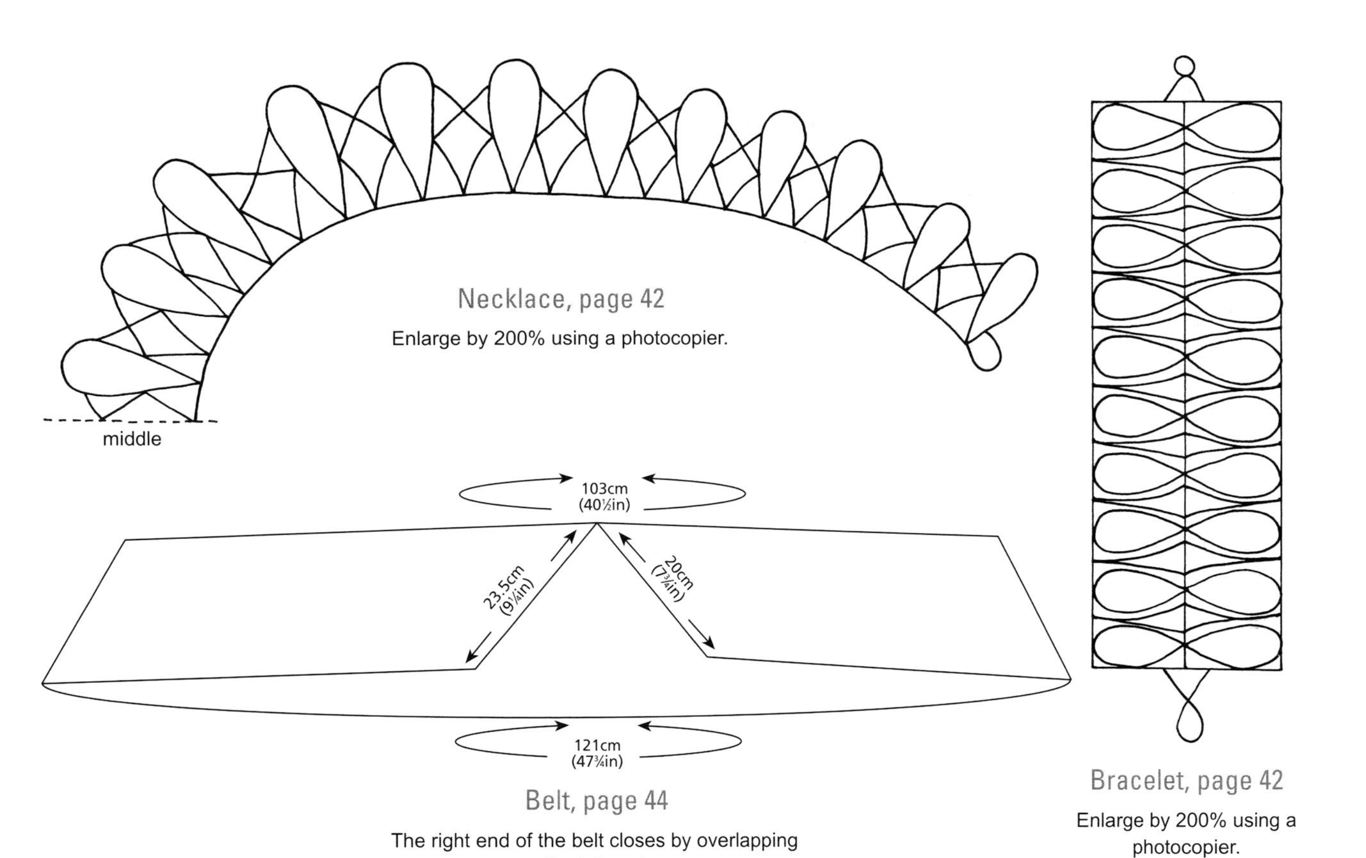

Necklace, page 42

Enlarge by 200% using a photocopier.

Belt, page 44

The right end of the belt closes by overlapping the left end.

Bracelet, page 42

Enlarge by 200% using a photocopier.

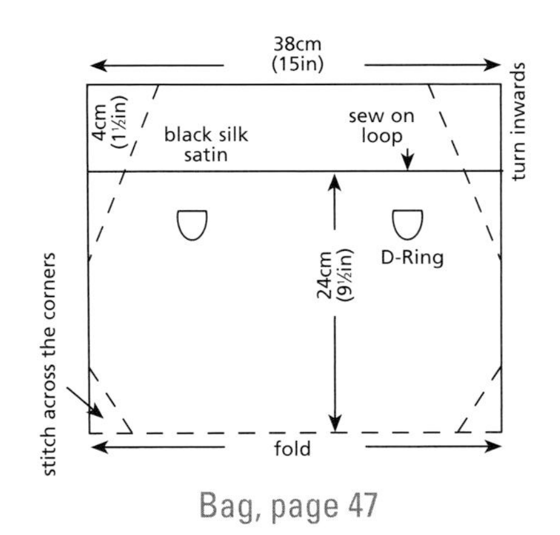

Bag, page 47

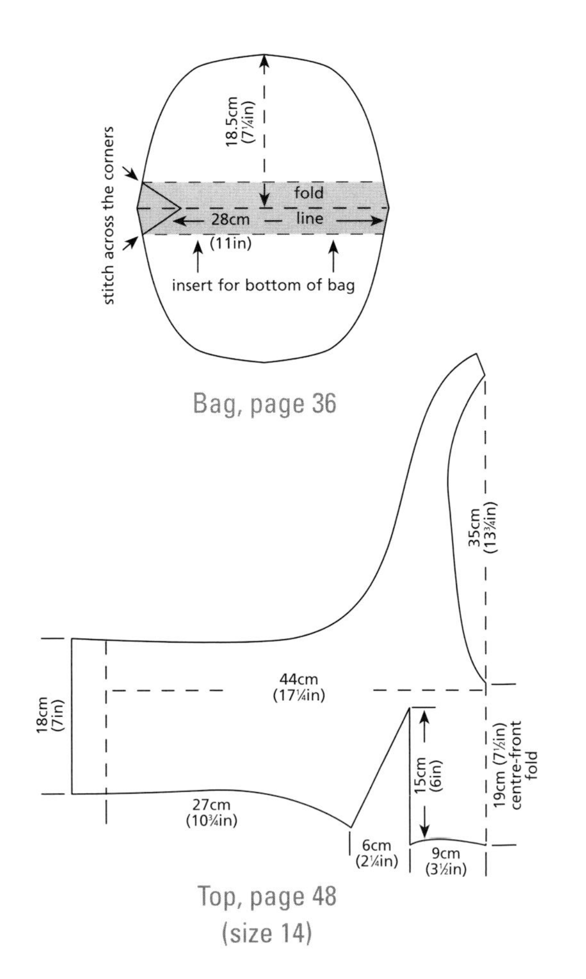

Bag, page 36

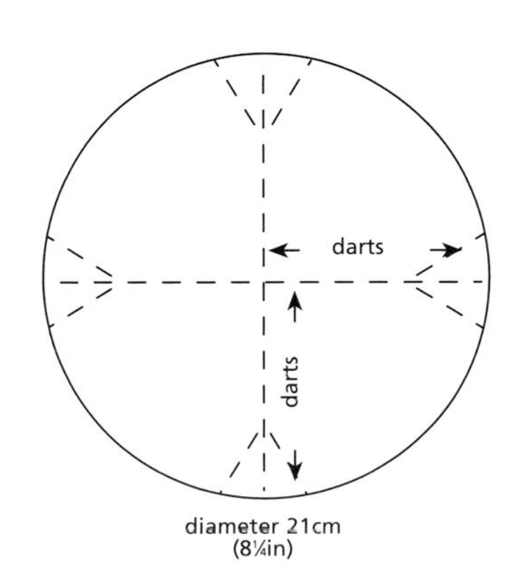

Cap, page 55

The finished top of the cap has a diameter of approx. 19cm (7½in).

Top, page 48
(size 14)

Manufacturers

Stabiliser:
Freudenberg Vliesstoffe KG, Heidelberg
www.vlieseline.de

Beads, sewing thread, jewellery accessories:
Gütermann Sulky®, Gutach
www.gutermann.com

Metallic embroidery thread, sewing threads, temporary spray adhesive, lamé yarn and metallic embroidery needles:
Madeira, Freiburg
www.madeira.de

Silk paints for steam-fixing:
Marabuwerke, Tamm
www.marabu-kreativ.de

Bag handles, Velcro® fastener, hooks and eyes, press studs and spray adhesive:
Prym Consumer, Stolberg
www.prym-consumer.de

Satin-silk chiffon stole – hand-rolled:
Schmidt & Bleicher, Marburg
www.ideen.com

The author would like to thank the companies listed above for their support.

Suppliers

If you have difficulty in obtaining any of the materials and equipment mentioned in this book, then please visit the Search Press website for details of suppliers:
www.searchpress.com

First published in Great Britain 2009 by Search Press Limited,
Wellwood, North Farm Road, Tunbridge Wells, Kent TN2 3DR

Originally published in Germany 2007 by
OZ-Verlags-GmbH

English translation by Cicero Translations

English edition edited and typeset by GreenGate Publishing
Services, Tonbridge, Kent

ISBN: 978-1-84448-433-1

Designs and production: Hannelore Koch
Editorial: Anke Sturm
Editing: Regina Sidabras
Photography: Christine Rosinski, apart from:
Hannelore Koch pages 11, 40, 55;
Uzwei Fotodesign pages 8–10
Styling: Biggi Hoheisel, apart from:
Dagmar Dobrofsky pages 12-17, 27, 45, 47, 53, 55;
Elke Reith pages 8–10
Layout design:
buchkonzept@web.de

Printed in Malaysia.